President Thomas Jefferson

Father of the Declaration of Independence

US History for Kids 3rd Grade

Children's American History

BABY PROFESSOR
EDUCATION KIDS

Speedy Publishing LLC

40 E. Main St. #1156

Newark, DE 19711

www.speedypublishing.com

In this book, we are going to talk about President Thomas Jefferson, before and after he became the third president of the United States. So let's get right to it!

THE EARLY LIFE OF THOMAS JEFFERSON

Thomas Jefferson was born on the 13th day of April in 1743 in Albemarie County, Virginia, which at the time was an English colony. He was the third of eight siblings, Peter and Jane, his parents, were very wealthy landowners. His mother was the daughter of a ship captain and planter by the name of Isham Randolph. She and her family had a high status in society. His father, Peter, was also a planter like his wife's father. His ancestors were of English origins.

THOMAS JEFFERSON

Thomas had many interests as a young boy. He loved reading and studying. He also loved to explore nature and play the violin. At the age of nine, he attended a school run by a minister from Scotland. There, he developed a love of languages and learned Greek and Latin as well as French. He had a thirst for knowledge and would study for up to fifteen hours a day.

Unfortunately, he was only fourteen years old when his father died. He inherited his father's lands and slaves. At the young age of 21, he began to manage these properties. Thanks to the guardianship of friends of his family he was able to continue his education.

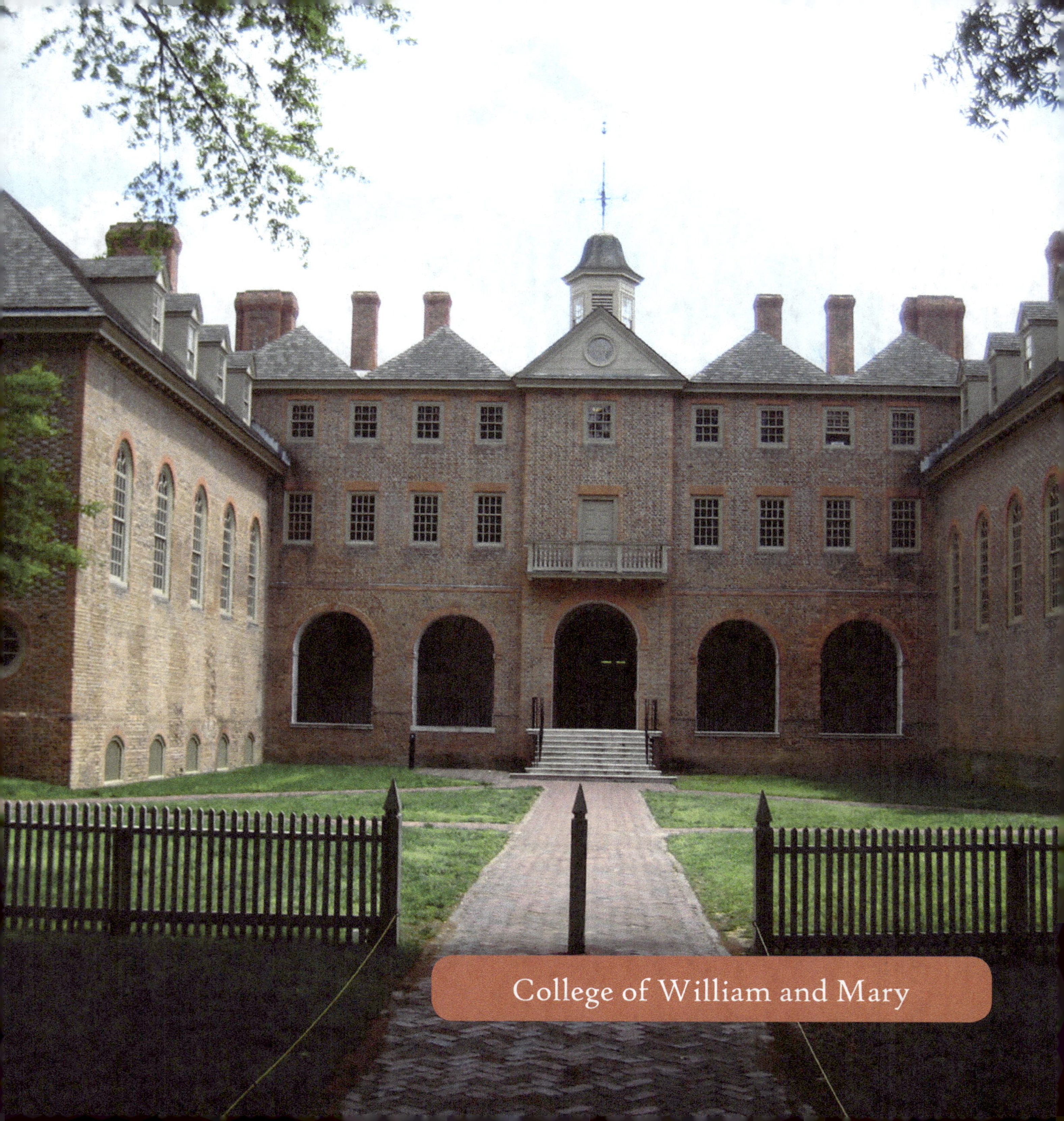
College of William and Mary

THOMAS JEFFERSON'S EDUCATION

Jefferson enrolled in the prestigious College of William and Mary in Virginia. He studied many different subjects including philosophy, metaphysics and mathematics. He studied the works of Locke, Bacon and Newton and later said that he felt these three men where the most important men the world had known.

At college he met a man by the name of George Wythe who would become influential in his life. Wythe was a law professor and Jefferson became interested in becoming a lawyer. He graduated with high honors and in 1767, at the age of 24, he was admitted to the Virginia Bar and began to practice law.

GEORGE WYTHE

College of William and Mary

He remained involved with the College of William and Mary throughout his life and helped to create the nation's first student honor code.

While Jefferson was in college he joined a secret club called the Flat Hat Club. He ate his meals in the community hall and said his prayers in the chapel. His life wasn't all serious though. He attended parties given by the governor. He continued to play the violin for enjoyment and developed a taste for fine wines.

THOMAS JEFFERSON STATUE

Thomas Jefferson was tall with sandy-colored hair and freckles. He was a fine speaker although he wouldn't have considered himself to be an orator. He was an eloquent and persuasive writer.

VIRGINIA HOUSE OF REPRESENTATIVES

Before he became the third president of the United States, Jefferson managed his huge estate as a farmer. He farmed tobacco as well as other crops. He was also a practicing lawyer. He first became a politician when he was elected to serve in the Virginia House of Representatives at the age of 26. He quickly became associated with George Washington and Patrick Henry.

THOMAS JEFFERSON

He started construction of a new home at Monticello just outside Charlottesville, Virginia on the 5,000 acres he had inherited. It is located on a hill and the word "monticello" comes from the Italian words for "little mount." This beautiful plantation home is now a national landmark.

On January 1 in 1772, he married Martha Wayles Skelton. His new wife was pretty, cultured, and had become a widow at a very young age. Her first husband was a wealthy plantation owner. She was five years younger than Jefferson. They eventually had six children together during Martha's short life, but only two of their children reached adulthood.

THOMAS JEFFERSON

In 1773, Martha's father passed away and Jefferson inherited his land as well as a huge amount of debt.

A NEW COUNTRY

By the 1770s, Virginia and the other colonies were beginning to feel that the British government wasn't treating them fairly. The Stamp Act and other acts of taxation had caused a lot of unrest. Jefferson helped to lead the fight for independence from Britain and was a representative for Virginia during the first Continental Congress.

The Continental Congress was a meeting of representatives from all of the thirteen American colonies. The men who were representatives from the colonies eventually served as the government of the United States during the Revolutionary War against Britain.

The First Continental Congress took place in 1774. The representatives, including Jefferson, took two important first steps. They sent a letter to King George III explaining their dissatisfaction with the way the colonies were being ruled. They asked for the end to the punishing laws that were passed after the Boston Tea Party. Then they made it clear that they would fight if the laws were not repealed.

KING GEORGE III

THE SECOND CONTINENTAL CONGRESS

During the Second Continental Congress, at the age of 33, Thomas Jefferson wrote the Declaration of Independence with help from other influential delegates, such as Benjamin Franklin and John Adams. This declaration basically stated that the colonies were going to create their own country and govern themselves. They were willing to fight to separate themselves from the British government.

The American Revolutionary War took place between 1775-1783. During this conflict, Jefferson continued to be an important leader and a founding father of the new country. He served many important positions. He was the US Minister to France after Benjamin Franklin and he was the governor of Virginia for two years. He became Secretary of State during George Washington's presidency and he was Vice President for John Adams during his term as the second president.

PRESIDENTIAL CANDIDATE
AARON BURR

THE UNITED STATES

In 1779, Jefferson was elected to be governor in his state of Virginia. During his term he wrote a famous bill on religious freedom that was made into law in 1786.

In 1782, Jefferson's wife died at the age of 34 just weeks after giving birth to their sixth child. She asked him to promise her that he would never marry again—a promise that he kept. Jefferson was destroyed by her death and wandered around his plantation. He was unable to speak clearly to his children because of his grief.

GEORGE WASHINGTON

After the Revolutionary War, in 1785, Jefferson became minister to France and became sympathetic to the revolutionists who were fighting there. In 1789, George Washington appointed Jefferson to be Secretary of State. Due to political differences with other cabinet members about the role of government, Jefferson resigned this post in 1793.

This clash led to the formation of two parties. Alexander Hamilton, the first Secretary of the Treasury, led the Federalists and Jefferson along with James Madison became leaders of the Democratic-Republicans, which is a different party than the

political parties we think of as Democrats and Republicans in the United States today. Jefferson wanted the states to have more power than the federal government and strongly opposed the platform of the Federalists.

JOHN ADAMS

RUN FOR THE PRESIDENCY

Jefferson ran to become the second president of the United States but was defeated by John Adams in 1796. He was appointed to be vice president instead. After John Adams completed his term, Jefferson was elected the third president of the United States in 1800. He and Aaron Burr received an equal number of electoral votes, so the House of Representatives made the final decision.

One of the first things Jefferson did in office was decrease the federal budget and give power back to the states. He also decreased taxes, which made him popular.

THOMAS JEFFERSON

RESTAURANT

During his two terms as president, Jefferson accomplished a great deal. He bought a huge section of land west of the colonies for the United States from the head of France, Napoleon. He bought this land, which nearly doubled the area of the US, for just 15 million dollars. This transaction was called the Louisiana Purchase.

Much of the land wasn't settled, so Jefferson enlisted the explorers Lewis and Clark to make an expedition and report on this western territory. He also sent ships from the US Navy to battle pirates on the coast of North Africa. The pirates had been attacking American ships that carried goods and he was determined to stop it. This led to the first Barbary War. During his second term, Jefferson kept the United States out of the European Napoleonic Wars.

JEFFERSON'S RETIREMENT AND DEATH

He retired to his home at Monticello to work on plans for the University of Virginia in 1819. The opening of this great university was a lifetime dream for him. The world of knowledge and ideas was always important to him and he wanted others to benefit from education as he had. It was the largest such project in the United States at that time and it was built upon a library, instead of a church. Jefferson was a firm believer in the separation of church and state.

Jefferson passed away on July 4, 1826, which was the 50th anniversary of the Declaration of Independence. John Adams also passed away on that day.

THOMAS JEFFERSON

Thomas Jefferson is considered to be one of the most intelligent presidents in the history of the United States. His views on freedoms for the individual, the separation of church and state, and the importance of education still have an influence on America and the world today. There are monuments named after him and his image appears on US currency.

Awesome! Now you know more about the life of President Thomas Jefferson, one of the Founding Fathers of the United States. You can find more History books from Baby Professor by searching the website of your favorite book retailer.

Visit

BABY PROFESSOR
EDUCATION KIDS

www.BabyProfessorBooks.com

to download Free Baby Professor eBooks
and view our catalog of new and exciting
Children's Books